Napa Valley

the Land, the Wine, the People

Charles O'Rear

essays by
Janice Fuhrman

foreword by
Robert and Margrit Mondavi

Wineviews Publishing, St. Helena

Ten Speed Press
Berkeley • Toronto

Napa Valley

Bruno Bartolucci

Contents

Foreword

Napa Valley means many things to many people—from the scenery with the fabulous vineyards surrounded by rolling hills, to the landscape bathed in an almost perfect climate. What also makes it special is certainly the cornucopia of food and the people creating the ambiance of this magnificent land.

Whatever this valley means to you, it can be found in the superb photography of our friend and neighbor, Charles O'Rear. Charles shows us scenes, views, and the innermost spirit that you rarely see in print.

Wine takes us to many parts of the world; we see new lands, taste new food and wine, and make new friends. However, we always return to Napa Valley with great joy because we love it very much. Our hearts and souls are planted in this soil. Here, every season has its enchanting changes.

We have known Charles for more than twenty years. We have read and seen all of his lovely books, but this new opus is a special moment for us. In this book Charles has expressed his passion for Napa Valley. His uncanny, keen eye has once more focused on what makes Napa Valley an extraordinary place. This time he has documented the valley's prized possessions—the grape growers—the folks who till the soil, who tend and plant the grapes. These classic portraits express the passion and the vision of the people who lovingly tend the vines.

In this book, you will encounter strong and majestic winery doors . . . an array of grape leaves . . . fog gathering over the misty valley . . . winery architecture . . . lifestyles . . . harvest . . . a romantic tour through wine cellars . . . frost-covered vines, and much more. Charles captures the unusual, the essence.

With much pride, we welcome you to this extraordinary book.

— Robert and Margrit Mondavi

Left: Vines of Smith-Madrone Vineyards frame the foreground of Mt. St. Helena, a 4,343-foot mountain northeast of Napa Valley.

Preceding pages: A sunrise fog hangs over Napa Valley from Spring Mountain *(pages 2–3)*. The rock formations of "stag's leap" rise behind an autumn vineyard of Stag's Leap Wine Cellars north of Napa *(pages 4–5)*. Antique bottles dating back to Prohibition show their age in a corner of a valley cave *(pages 6–7)*. Hands of ninety-four-year-old immigrant Feliciana Nava of Napa *(page 8)*. Grower Bruno Bartolucci poses during a break in his St. Helena vineyard *(page 9)*. Chardonnay grapes wait for crushing by a home winemaker *(pages 10–11)*. Grape leaves and clusters accent the gates of Gianni Paoletti Winery, along the Silverado Trail near Calistoga *(page 12)*.

Introduction

No matter where I've been, every time I drive into Napa Valley I feel that I've reached the most beautiful and most perfect spot on earth. I breathe deeply. More than anywhere on earth, all of my senses come alive here—the smells, the air, the tastes, the sounds, the touch, the views. Is it possible for anybody to love a place so much?

My photography career, mostly with *National Geographic* magazine, has taken me to twenty-five countries and all fifty states. In the pursuit of that career, I have flown two million miles—I've hiked the Alps, camped in Siberia, hunted alligators in Louisiana swamps, shared meals with New Guinea village chiefs, and crossed the wild animal kingdoms of South Africa. Yet there is no other place on this earth that feeds my heart and soul as much as Napa Valley. This is why I have called Napa Valley my home since *National Geographic* sent me here on assignment more than two decades ago.

Today the valley attracts people like myself—people who love to drink great wine, savor wonderful foods, experience the moderate Mediterranean climate, share life's experiences with each other, or simply want to live in a visually gorgeous rural setting. It is a happy place.

With each day I see the valley unfold with new surprises. And each day I find more to love. From my home surrounded by vineyards at the edge of St. Helena, I awake to a sunrise over the eastern hills, to a land silver with dew, to a vast sea of vines I can reach out and touch. There are few sounds here, except for an occasional passing breeze drifting in from the Pacific Ocean thirty miles away. This place—so removed from the rest of today's hurried world—feels majestic and powerful one moment, serene and peaceful the next.

Above: Swiss immigrant Anton Nichelini poses in his vineyard in 1929. His grandson, Joseph, a stockbroker in Napa, continues the family tradition of growing grapes east of St. Helena. Portraits of grape growers are featured throughout this book.

For me, the town of St. Helena is familiar. It is the size of the town where I grew up in rural western Missouri. So, I've returned home in a way—to a place where few lock their doors, where people dress casually, where I see familiar faces when I do my daily errands. But it's also a place where I can meet friends for dinner at a world-class restaurant and drink

extraordinary wine.

For this book I have chosen to take you deep inside the heart of this valley—down winding country lanes, into lush green vineyards, up rocky mountain sides, through wild canyons tucked away in the hills. Here you will see the simple beauty of grape leaves, the faces, hands, and body language of the growers, the artistically crafted doors of wineries, and the splendid vistas that are transformed—as through the changing colored lenses of a camera—from brilliant yellows to oranges to reds and finally to midnight blues as each day moves into night. As you turn the pages, you will make many discoveries and you will see why this valley is like no other in this world.

The European immigrants who came here many years ago and the Victorian architecture that was built during the California Gold Rush play an important part in the valley today. Yet while the valley continues to embrace the old, it has embraced the new, too—new foods, new styles of wine and winery architecture, new homes, new friends.

I have made many friends here and they have graciously opened their homes and their lives to me, breathed life into my images, and shared something of themselves and this place. I owe this book to them.

— Charles O'Rear

Left and above: Autumn descends on opposite ends of the valley as frost outlines grape leaves near Calistoga and a shadow falls on a barn in the Carneros region in southern Napa County, at the north end of the San Francisco Bay.

Following pages: Winter fog silhouettes a vineyard and velvet ash trees along Highway 29 in Rutherford. Temperatures cooled and heated by a mixture of penetrating sunshine and ocean air from the bay thirty miles south provide ideal conditions for grapevines

Alchemy &

Abundance

*N*apa Valley vintners are masters of transforming something ordinary—the grape—into something precious—wine. From Europe to the western edge of the New World, generations of vintners have performed their magic on the simple grape, each building on the knowledge of the last. But every potion, whether magical or mundane, begins with its ingredients and the essence of any wine is the fruit of the vine. Before all the recognition, the lavish food and wine offerings, the imposing architecture and kingly art collections, there was simply this breathtaking long, narrow valley and there were the grape growers, the first wave of whom reached the Napa Valley in the mid-nineteenth century. They were men and women who came from Italy, from other parts of Europe, and from the bleak white winters of eastern and midwestern states. They came because they heard Napa Valley was a fruitful land, in whose rich soil anything could grow. They dreamed of abundance and they reaped it: fruits and vegetables, nuts, fish plucked from the surging Napa River. But what few of them envisioned was that they would become growers of the noble grapes that would give life to some of the world's best wines. Today, in this land of plenty, grape growers, winemakers, and field workers labor together to invent, and reinvent each year, the nectar that is Napa Valley.

Left: A vineyard on Petrified Forest Road near Calistoga shows signs of autumn. Grape leaves are deciduous, sometimes turning brilliant shades of yellow and red, before falling off every year.

Preceding page 28: A cluster of ripe cabernet sauvignon grapes will soon be picked and crushed to begin fermentation, the first step in the process of aging. Bottles of pinot noir and chardonnay juice await analyses at the laboratory of Mumm Napa Valley in St. Helena.

Above: Glowing barrels at Demptos Napa Cooperage receive "toasting" from burning oak chips. A popular winemaking practice today, toasted barrels give additional flavors to wines.

Right: In the Stags Leap district, threat of an early morning frost forces grape growers to light vineyard heaters. After spring "bud break," severe frost can destroy the year's crop and seriously damage vines.

Following pages: Rainwater settles in a winter vineyard and reflects the sky along Deer Park Road in St. Helena.

Left: Vine tentacles hang from a trellis wire during a midwinter rainstorm in a St. Helena vineyard.

Above: Widely spaced rows and "head pruned" vines stand like sentries at sunrise.

Following pages: Handwork plays an important role in grape growing. A bud cut from a cane of cabernet sauvignon is prepared for grafting onto rootstock. Grape grower Andy Rossi of St. Helena holds shears he has used for fifteen years to prune dormant canes from his petite sirah. He single-handedly plows, prunes, and cares for his three thousand vines many of which are nearly a hundred years old.

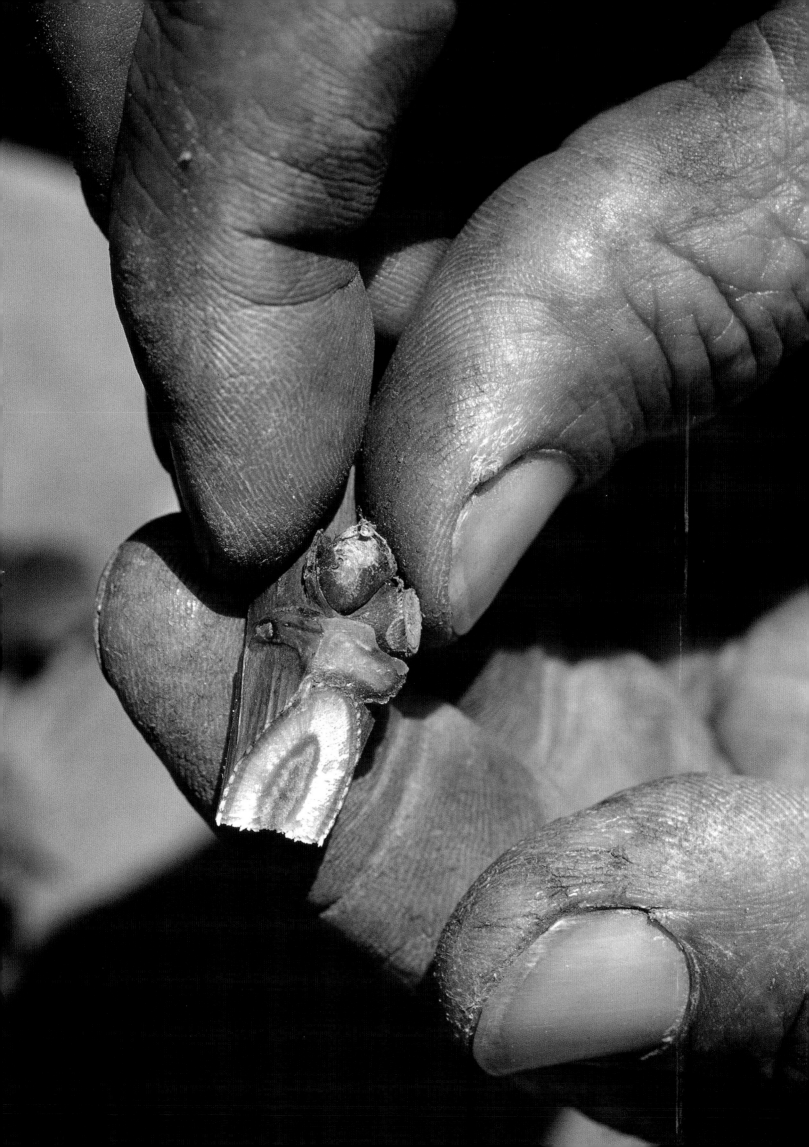

Andrew Rossi

Let us get up early to the vineyards;

let us see if the vine flourish,

whether the tender grape appear.

SONG OF SOLOMON 7:12

Right: A field-worker in Oakville carries pruned canes to a burn pile. Canes cut annually from grapevines will be burned, chopped, and recycled into the soil, or shaped into ornamental items such as baskets and wreaths.

Preceding pages: A dormant "head pruned" grenache vine, which may be fifty years old, stretches ten feet from tip to tip. The vines in this vineyard, as well as this style of pruning, are being replaced rapidly with vines producing more popular grapes, which are trained onto trellises. Trellises allow grapevines to reach higher and wider, thus giving more exposure to the sun.

Above and right: Spring heralds new vine growth at Barnett Vineyards on Spring Mountain. The two thousand-foot average elevation and cooler temperatures in this area cause grapes to mature later than on the floor of Napa Valley, where temperatures can reach 115 degrees. These delicate grape blooms on a cabernet vine will soon develop into a radiant cluster of grapes.

Preceding pages: Wild mustard announces the approach of spring in vineyards across Napa Valley. Locations of mustard are not predictable and can depend on soil and climate conditions of the previous year. These vines along the Silverado Trail have been trained in the style of "T-vine," a concept developed during the 1980s.

Pauline Tofanelli

For singing till his heaven fills,

'Tis love of earth that he instils,

And ever winging up and up,

Our valley is his golden cup,

And he the wine which overflows

To lift us with him as he goes.

GEORGE MEREDITH 1828–1909

Left and following pages 50–57: Today in the valley, grapes are grown mostly by corporations, while independent growers like Pauline Tofanelli *(left)* provide a style and quality of grapes sought by many wineries. Pauline and her sister, May, grow grapes on thirty acres on Dunaweal Lane near Calistoga. On the following pages, and throughout this book, is a portfolio of some of the valley's many growers. Most of them are not associated with a winery, but instead grow and sell the grapes independently. They are described on pages 226–227 of this book.

Miles Alexander

Chester Brandlin

Andy Beckstoffer

Salvador and Oscar Renteria

Aldo Biale

Henry "Irv" Tiedemann

Ed Chaix

Charles Wagner

Belle and Barney Rhodes

Paul Saviez

James Talcott

Mike Morisoli

James St. Clair

Angelo Regusci

Keith Bowers

Lindy Johnson

Grant Cairns

Earle Presten

Frank Takahashi

Martha and Tom May

James Frediani

Robert Keig

Ira Lee

Linda and Mike Neal

Roy Enderlin

Edgar Ilsley

Osvaldo Particelli

Fred Lyon

Bob Barbaris

Dorothy and Benito Barbozza

William Lincoln, Sr.

Wes Walker

Lewis Carpenter

Harold Varozza

Frank Perata

Arn Vallerga

Frank "Laurie" Wood

Craig Battuello

Jim Haire

Bill Bartolucci

Alex Vyborny

Claire and Bill Ballentine

Michael, Bill and John Hanna

Above: Morning dew clings to these chardonnay grapes waiting to be crushed at an Oakville winery. Many growers prefer to pick grapes in the early morning to take advantage of cool temperatures, which can produce more flavors.

Preceding pages: The terraces of Cain Vineyards on Spring Mountain provide a foreground to a sunrise over foggy Napa Valley. Hills in the distance stretch along the eastern side of the valley, with the highest peaks reaching nearly two thousand feet. The valley floor, below the fog, rises only a few hundred feet above sea level.

Above: Vineyards reach maturity in the rolling hills of Dollar Hide Ranch in Pope Valley, an eastern Napa County region. Grapes from these vines will go to St. Supéry Vineyards and Winery near Rutherford. Microclimates in Napa Valley have taken on an important role in determining where grapes will be planted.

Following pages: Leaves from many of Napa Valley's most popular grapevines look similar to the untrained eye. Normally, the juice from at least two or more grapes are blended to make wine.

Cabernet Sauvignon

Chardonnay

Sauvignon Blanc

Sangiovese

Merlot

Pinot Noir

Zinfandel

Petite Sirah

Oh, for a draught of vintage that hath been

Cool'd a long age in the deep delved earth,

Tasting of Flora and the country green,

Dance, and Provencal song, and sunburnt mirth!

JOHN KEATS 1795–1821

Right: Vineyards, trees, and mountains provide an artistic palette from the Silverado Trail. The Lombardy poplars have become more common in the valley as residents try to duplicate European landscapes of similar climates.

Following pages: Panoramic views from the hallways of Dominus Estate accentuate the linear landscape of its vineyards near Yountville. This Swiss-designed, French-owned winery brings a sleek, contemporary architectural presence to the valley.

Above: Winemaker Elias Fernandez samples Chardonnay from the cellars of Shafer Vineyards near Napa.

Right: The blending of wines from different vineyards is considered an art by many vintners. At Araujo Estate near Calistoga, winemaker Françoise Peschon consults with owners Bart and Daphne Araujo.

Following pages: Sampling wine from barrels at Stag's Leap Wine Cellars requires a siphon and the agile bodies of winemakers Michael Silacci and Julia Winiarski. The plastic tube used to siphon wine is appropriately named a "thief." Valley vintners began aging wine in oak barrels when interest in wine and new wineries increased in the 1960s and 1970s.

Above: Winemaker Chris Phelps uses a traditional French method with a "marteau tenaille" to extract wine for sampling.

Right: Round Hill winemaker Mark Swain is dwarfed by sixteen-foot tall oak tanks, holding up to 6,700 gallons of wine.

Following pages: A thousand oak barrels wind through the Grand Chai of Opus One in Oakville. Many wineries age wine in barrels from one to three years before bottling.

Places &

Passions

*N*apa Valley is widely known for its passions: a passion for the land and the bounty it produces, a passion for the mystical properties of wine, for fresh and vibrant food combinations that awaken the senses—an all-encompassing passion for the good life. Any visitor will notice immediately a passion for detail in the precise rows of sculpted vines edged in rosebushes, in the stands of olive trees with their silvery leaves glinting in sunlight, in the welcoming doors, many of them exquisitely carved, of Napa Valley wineries, and of course, in the vintages Napa Valley conjures, as if by magic, from soil, grapes, steel tanks, and barrels. There are big wineries with big names, and small, family-owned ones, whose wine you can taste and purchase only here. Each day in Napa Valley is a sensory pleasure. From the layered aromas and velvety texture of a ruby Cabernet Sauvignon and the warm mineral waters that shoot from the earth at the valley's north end, to the bright, intense flavors of wine country cuisine, each day in each season is a hedonist's delight. There are wineries here with museum-quality art collections, wineries that are themselves art pieces because of their striking architecture: Spanish mission, French château, Victorian, Tuscan, farmhouse, barn-style, and post-modern. They come with innovative gardens, and long views across acres of lush, emerald valley and hillside. Most important of all, behind each winery, gallery, or eatery there are the people— vintners, scientists, farmers, chefs, writers, and painters, all of whom will take the time to tell you the stories of how they came to fall in love with wine and with this valley.

Left: Beringer Vineyard's 1883 Rhine House in St. Helena echoes the era and homeland of German immigrant Frederick Beringer who arrived in America in the mid-1800s. It accommodates offices, retail selling, and wine tasting rooms for the Australian-owned winery.

Preceding page 76: Winter fog near Oakville surrounds a century-old water tower, a symbol of days past in the valley before modern water systems were installed. Ten miles north, in the town of St. Helena, a mural in the post office depicts harvest as interpreted in 1941 by artist Lew Keller. The painting was made with support of the federal government's Works Progress Administration (WPA).

Facing page: A view of two cellars—the barrel aging room at Cakebread Cellars and the ornate iron gates guarding the underground cellar of Far Niente Winery's Dolce, a late-harvest wine produced with semillon and sauvignon blanc grapes.

This page: Fall colors frame a window at Chateau Montelena near Calistoga *(right)*, and the front of the Niebaum-Coppola Estate Winery in Rutherford *(above)*. The winery was built in 1887 by Gustave Niebaum, a Finnish sea captain, and was purchased in 1995 by movie director Francis Ford Coppola. Niebaum's great grandniece, Robin Lail, produces wine today in Napa Valley.

Following pages: Doors convey extraordinary significance as wineries in Napa Valley search for icons to welcome visitors. Many depict arches reflecting the round shapes found in winemaking—from tunnels, to barrels, to bottles. The opening doors of the gatefold lead into the winery of Grace Family Vineyards in St. Helena. It was carved in 1987 by local artist David Voisard.

Screaming Eagle

Cosentino Winery

Grgich Hills

Freemark Abbey

Charles Krug Winery

Duckhorn Vineyards

Flora Springs

Edgewood Estate

Frank-Rombauer Cellars

Rutherford Hill

Mumm Napa Valley

Silverado Vineyards

Louis M. Martini

Milat Vineyards

Harlan Estate

Far Niente

PlumpJack

Sutter Home

Araujo Estate

Pine Ridge

Opus One

Cuvaison Winery

Chimney Rock Winery

Hess Collection

Beaulieu Vineyard

Rutherford Grove

Saintsbury

Beringer Vineyards

V. Sattui Winery

Clos Pegase

Chateau Montelena

Peju Province

Rudd Vineyards and Winery

Carneros Creek

Clos Du Val

Domaine Carneros

Napa Wine Company

Left: Lattice allows sun into the open air courtyard of Artesa Winery near Napa. The winery was designed by Spanish architect Domingo Triay and Napa Valley architect Earl R. Bouligny, and built in 1991 as Codorniu Napa. It was renamed Artesa in 1999 although ownership remains with the Raventos family of Barcelona, who are sixteenth generation winemakers.

Above and following pages 90–91: Visitors to the atrium of Clos Pegase winery near Calistoga see a reverse view of the entry *(above)*. The innovative winery is owned by Jan Shrem and was designed by architect Michael Graves and built in 1987.

Following pages 92–93: The rock and steel cage walls of ultramodern Dominus Estate winery in Yountville form an illusory pyramid against the summer sky. Swiss architects Herzog and de Meuron designed the building for French owner Christian Moueix. It houses winemaking facilities, barrel storage, and offices.

Left: A classic "parterre" garden covers the Chardonnay cellars at Newton Vineyards above St. Helena. The garden was designed in 1981 by Peter Newton. The winery is owned by Peter and Su Hua Newton.

Above: The garden entrance to the French Laundry restaurant in Yountville also takes advantage of the Mediterranean climate, which produces moderate temperatures most of the year. French Laundry, which has received much national recognition, is one of a dozen restaurants attracting visitors to the valley.

Preceding pages: The "hemispheric" form of Opus One, Oakville, becomes apparent from this aerial view of the winery. Los Angeles architect Scott Johnson describes Opus One as "introverted, like a jewel box." The Grand Chai of barrels lies under the semicircular grassy berm. Offices and reception rooms occupy the stone buildings at top. Built in 1991, Opus One is owned jointly by the Robert Mondavi family of Napa Valley and Baroness Philippine de Rothschild of Bordeaux.

Above: Visitors to Artesa Winery near Napa are welcomed by this sculpture by Barcelona artist Marcel Martí.

Right: A weathered steel sculpture, *Chi*, graces the garden of Brix, a restaurant near Yountville. Sculptor, winemaker, and attorney Richard Mendelson of Napa provided art pieces for a summer exhibition at the restaurant.

Following pages 100–101: Reminiscent of a French château, the winery of Domaine Carneros is located along Highway 12, west of Napa. After visiting this region as a child, Claude Taittinger, president of Champagne Taittinger of France, returned in the 1980s to build this winery, which produces primarily sparkling wines.

Following pages 102–103: The daytime wait staff of Bistro Don Giovanni, north of Napa, listen to Chef de Cuisine Angela Lee describe the day's specials. The restaurant opened in 1993.

Top: Giant flower arrangements greet visitors to
Bistro Don Giovanni. The Napa Valley climate and access
to the San Francisco Flower Mart enable professional
flower arrangers to design spectacular displays.

Above: Colorful displays also come with food,
such as these fresh chiles held by Isaac Perez who has
prepared food for farmworkers for many years.

Top: Summer sunshine inspires an employee to
bring tomatoes outside to be dried with salt at Tra Vigne
restaurant, St. Helena. The result will be "tomato conserva,"
an ingredient in foods served in the restaurant.
In 1987, Tra Vigne opened next to an abandoned
sherry winery, now the Cantinetta.

Above: Server Paul Moxie holds a "Grand Plateau" of
seafoods at Bouchon in Yountville. Decor of the restaurant
is patterned after a French bistro.

Left, above and right: St. Helena Farmer's Market, which runs from spring through fall, provides a dazzling array of food and flowers. The Friday morning market serves the upper Napa Valley, while the City of Napa holds twice-weekly markets for the lower valley. Visitors to the market include locals, tourists, and newcomers who have built second homes in the towns and rural areas surrounding Calistoga, St. Helena, Rutherford, Oakville, and Yountville.

Left: History and location play important roles in distinguishing the valley from other rural settings. Architecture of the wineries, commercial buildings, and homes has been influenced by the European immigrants who live here, the proximity to San Francisco, and the miners who came here after the California Gold Rush of 1849. Ornate light fixtures welcome visitors to downtown St. Helena. The city bought the "electroliers" (electric & chandeliers) in 1915 at the Panama-Pacific International Exposition in San Francisco.

Above: Oakville Grocery sells specialty foods from this building along Highway 29. The business has operated continuously since 1881, mostly as a "mercantile" store and since the 1970s as a popular spot for day visitors.

Top: Diners at Brannan's Grill in Calistoga
experience the outdoors when windows are opened to
the sidewalks of Lincoln Street. The restaurant is named after
Sam Brannan, who developed Calistoga in the 1860s.

Above: A menu awaits guests at Auberge du Soleil, a resort
and restaurant in the eastern hills overlooking the valley.

Top: Bistro Jeanty, named after chef/owner
Phillipe Jeanty, opened in 1998 and displays a facade of lights
and stripes in Yountville. The number of hotel rooms in
the town has doubled in four years, and several restaurants
have opened during the same period.

Above: The stone walls of an 1884 building enclose
the restaurant Terra in St. Helena. The Taylor, Duckworth & Co.
foundry building has been placed on the national register
of historical places by the U.S. Department of the Interior.
For many years it served as a chicken hatchery.

Facing page: Interest in olives has risen dramatically in the past decade, adding to the harmony of wine and food. Olive trees grow heartily in the Mediterranean climate of the Napa Valley and the fruit is flavor filled. From cured and seasoned whole olives to olive oil, the demand continues. Bottles at Harrison Napa Valley, St. Helena, show stylized olive trees. Olives headed for oil get poured into Harrison's one hundred-year-old granite press from Italy.

This page: Arlene Bernstein of Napa fills boxes with just-picked olives on their way to become pressed into oil for personal consumption. In St. Helena, Leonora Particelli hangs the Italian flag from her family-owned Napa Valley Olive Oil Mfg. Company. The one-time cattle barn and olive oil pressing plant built nearly a hundred years ago now sells locally grown olives and a variety of specialty foods.

Above: The Napa Valley Wine Train transports more than 100,000 tourists a year from Napa to St. Helena and offers passengers gourmet dining along with a scenic tour. A hundred years ago it was a route for tourists coming from San Francisco to valley spas and country homes. The Southern Pacific Railroad carried freight to the upper valley as late as the 1980s, and in 1987 the right-of-way was purchased by the Wine Train.

Right: Resembling a set of train tracks is a display of wines that attracts shoppers at Dean and DeLuca Market near St. Helena.

Facing page, top: A tall, slender bottle accompanies its owner to an annual "Bring Your Own Magnum" event at a St. Helena restaurant. The party is sponsored by *Wine Spectator* magazine in conjunction with the annual Napa Valley Wine Auction.

Facing page, bottom: Brother Timothy Diener, FSC, stands in vineyards once owned by Christian Brothers near Napa where he began making the valley famous in the 1960s with his national television appearances. The bell tower of Mont LaSalle, once an icon for the religious winemakers, appears in the distance.

This page: Bidding for wine is a popular pastime, especially at the annual Napa Valley Wine Auction *(right)* and Home Winemakers Classic *(above).*

Preceding pages: Since 1978 hot air balloons ascending
from bases near Yountville have become popular attractions
for tourists. As many as 20,000 visitors will take rides
yearly from the valley floor. Area weather patterns require
morning flights for balloons in this area. This balloon
drifts over a widely spaced vineyard near the Veteran's
Home of California in Yountville.

Left: Newlyweds pose for a photographer at Meadowood Resort, St. Helena. Attracted by a winery setting, up to a dozen or more couples choose to tie the knot on summer weekends throughout Napa Valley.

Above: Golfers move along the greens of Silverado Country Club and Resort in Napa. Silverado's two popular eighteen-hole courses are home to the Transamerica Tournament, a senior PGA Tour event.

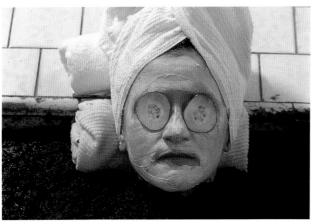

Facing page: Date palms and a "southern mansion" façade distinguish the main entrance of Silverado Country Club and Resort. The "Spa" at Silverado opened in 1999. It is 16,000 square feet with a 25-meter lap pool and private treatment rooms.

Above and following pages: Hot mineral water soothes guests under cover in the jet pool at the Calistoga Spa Hot Springs. Century-old wells heated from thermal activity provide spas with hot water and high mineral content.

Left: A guest at Dr. Wilkinson's Hot Springs Resort in Calistoga soaks in volcanic ash and peat heated with hot springs water. Cucumbers and a facial masque cover her face.

Above: A competitor in a 10K run at the St. Helena Hometown Harvest Festival passes autumn vineyards on Fir Hill Drive.

Right: At Auberge du Soleil, on the valley's eastern slopes, a swimmer glides across the resort's pool.

Facing page: Napa Valley is home to a colorful array of winemakers and enthusiasts. Here, home winemaker Jerry Hyde of St. Helena pours grapes into a plastic container in his backyard. He and friends climb into the container and crush grapes with their feet. His turn-of-the century water tower looms behind him. The shirt of John Thoreen, the "Wine Tutor" at Meadowood Resort, displays labels of California wineries. He presents wine seminars and events appealing to beginners and connoisseurs.

This page: Charity wine tastings occur regularly in the valley and guests can often take the wine glass they use as a souvenir. A guest at a wine tasting leaves with a full pocket. Server Mario Traverso balances twenty-five wine glasses from the dishwasher to the dining room at the Wine Spectator Greystone restaurant, at the campus of the Culinary Institute of America in St. Helena.

Left: Like an umbrella protecting the occupants, a date palm tree hangs over the Wappo Bar & Bistro in Calistoga.

Above and following pages: Graduates of a baking and pastry class from the Culinary Institute of America, St. Helena campus, pose in front of the school's building. The school has taught as many as four thousand students annually since it opened here in 1995.

Left: On a foggy, winter morning the entrance to
a St. Helena home displays the name of the owner's
winery. The house was built in 1910 by the Spotts
family, hence the name.

Above: After the fog burns off, a fresh bouquet
greets visitors who tour the Frog's Leap Winery
near Rutherford.

Seasons &

Celebrations

*T*here is much to behold during each season in Napa Valley. In winter, the grapevines are pruned and tied, the soil prepared, and the sprawling vineyards glow with golden mustard plants. In spring, when the frosty earth reawakens, there is planting and fertilizing and a renewed sense of hope about this year's crop as the land turns green and tiny flowers appear on the vine where later there will be berries. A summer flurry of activity follows as crops are thinned, vines trained, and berries sampled. At harvest, the valley shimmers in reds, golds, and oranges and pours forth the fruits of the yearlong labors. Working under a baking late summer sun, or in the sludge of fall rains, field workers yield plump red and white grapes, the beginnings of the elixir that is Napa Valley wine. While vineyards are tended, winemakers look searchingly into the sky and worry about rain—too much or too little—about vine pests and disease and fires, the calamities of nature this valley submits to each year. Vintners are risk takers, and their faith in the land is rewarded by the joyful occasions people celebrate here, a kaleidoscope of events fashioned year-round to give thanks for the rich soil, temperate climate, and the boundless energy of the workers. We revel in what the earth brings forth, taking the time to rejoice in the bounty of an upcoming harvest or savoring bottles from harvests past. Music, food, wine, and flowers are present at every gathering, simple or grand, large or small. Whether a charity black-tie gala under a dreamy summer night sky or a blue-jeans-and-T-shirt barbecue with lively mariachi music, the generous spirit of Napa Valley marks each as an unforgettable moment in time.

Left: When the harvest begins, so does the hard work. Headlights illuminate the way for a mechanical harvester through morning fog in a vineyard near the Napa River. Harvesting for most premium wine grapes is done by hand.

Preceding page 138: Cabernet sauvignon grapes appear ready to burst with juice as they ripen before harvest. After several years of aging, the grapes will be transformed to wine and poured at many a table such as this one *(below)* at a Meadowood Resort wedding reception.

Following pages: A forty-pound box of cabernet sauvignon grapes is carried to a nearby gondola.

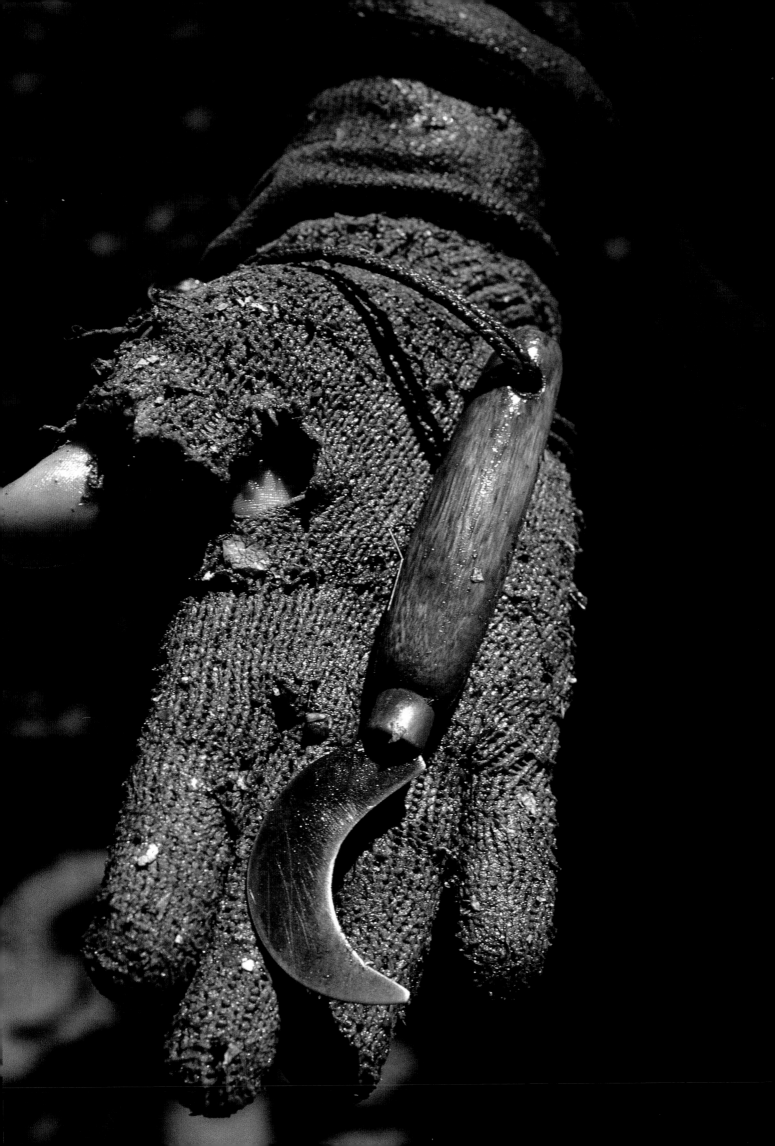

Right: A coast live oak frames the sun rising over vineyards near Oakville. In the peak growing season of midsummer, warm days and cool nights can cause vines to grow as much as an inch a day.

Preceding pages 144–145: A gloved hand provides some protection from the hooked knife used to cut grape bunches in Napa Valley vineyards. A fast worker can harvest as many as three tons a day and, on a great day, earn as much as $300 for the work. A woman in a St. Helena vineyard offers a smile as she waits to receive grapes from fellow pickers.

Preceding pages 146–147: Harvesting at Araujo Estate near Calistoga, a picker breathes the cool night air. Generated lights pulled through the vineyard in the early morning hours provide the only illumination. As prices and demand for wine increases so does the need for higher quality grapes. As a result, some growers begin picking in the night to maximize flavors in the fruit.

Preceding pages 148–149: Autumn vineyards surround a wind machine as seen from the air north of Yountville. The threat of spring frosts makes these machines necessary.

Above and right: A winery building of V. Sattui in
St. Helena echos the colors of picking boxes filled
with pinot noir grapes at Mumm Napa Valley along the
Silverado Trail. Manager Jim O'Shea inspects the fruit
before crushing. Many wineries have begun using small
boxes to minimize damage to grapes, though some still
utilize large gondolas that can carry up to five tons of
the fruit.

Soren Bloch

Bruno Solari

Randy and Scott Snowden

Ted Tamagni

Ted Laurent

Tom Kenefick

Top: Worn gloves are testimony to the strenuous work
required to move barrels by hand. Most wine barrels used in
Napa Valley are made from oak and hold approximately
sixty gallons. Barrels this size allow more wood to make contact
with the aging wine, producing richer flavors.

Above: Vineyard owner Bruno Bartolucci is exhausted but
happy after a day of plowing his St. Helena vineyard.

Top: After a day of picking, workers pause with their boxes. Ripe grapes have as much as 25 percent sugar, which makes for sticky and wet work. Many pickers in Napa Valley come from the Mexican state of Michoacán and go home after fall harvest. They return to the valley for winter pruning.

Above: A picker's tools—a curved knife, gloves, and a box—take a break in a Carneros vineyard.

Left: During harvest, Main Street of St. Helena becomes a pipeline of grapes as trucks move through the town headed to nearby wineries. The 108-year-old Ritchie building, an icon for downtown St. Helena, is a backdrop for this traditional gondola carrying sauvignon blanc grapes.

Above: Employees from the Screaming Eagle winery near Oakville end a summer day with bocce ball, an Italian sport introduced to the valley in the 1980s.

Top: Used wine barrels fill The Barrel Shop, a recycling
yard in American Canyon south of Napa. A few wineries use
barrels only once, but wineries typically use a barrel for
several years until the interior wood no longer gives flavors.
Here the barrels will be sold to either home winemakers
or cut into ornamental garden containers.

Above: At Miller Vineyards near Yountville,
empty, clean gondolas are upended to dry in the sun after
the annual fall harvest.

Top: Wine bottles of the past form a decorative wall at Heitz
Wine Cellar in St. Helena. Because of the increased popularity
of wines over the past forty years, it has become more efficient
to standardize bottle shapes reflecting wines of Bordeaux
(high neck) and wines of Burgundy (tapered neck).

Above: Glasses waiting to be filled with sparkling wine line
a reception table at an Oakville winery.

Above: A rolling vineyard near Calistoga shows how symmetry plays an important role in the valley. This vineyard, Rattlesnake Acres, is owned by grower Roy Enderlin, who named his land in 1975 after he found twenty-four snakes in one year. The steep slope allows him to drive a tractor in only one direction—up.

Preceding pages: Rows of sparkling wine bottles await customers at Domaine Chandon. Built in 1977, before county laws restricted wineries from serving food, it is one of the few that also boasts a restaurant. The term "sparkling wine" is used by most producers in the United States because "Champagne" is a registered name for the same drink that comes from the French region of Champagne, east of Paris.

Above: Predictable weather allows residents to plan many outdoor celebrations like this afternoon luncheon near Yountville.

Following pages: A sea of yellow covers the ground in front of Beaulieu Vineyard in Rutherford. Overnight rain knocked turning leaves from these velvet ash trees. Beaulieu began operation as a winery in 1900 and its wines were some of the first in Napa Valley to be recognized nationally.

Above: A charity dinner is served at tables around
the pool of Garen and Shari Staglin, owners of Staglin
Family Vineyard, near Oakville.

Right: Chamber music is performed alfresco at the
Spottswoode Winery owner's home in St. Helena.
A series of summer concerts, "Music in the Vineyards," is
featured at various valley wineries and homes every year.

Following pages: Red skies and a fiery sunrise silhouette
the cupola of Patrick O'Dell's Turnbull Wine Cellars near
Rutherford. Recent forest fires one hundred miles north
intensified the sky's color.

Top: Server Larry Nadeau makes last-minute
preparations for guests at the French Laundry restaurant in
Yountville. The nationally acclaimed restaurant gets
its name from a former "French Steam Laundry" built
on the site more than one hundred years ago.

Above: Visitors to Merryvale Vineyard's cask room
in St. Helena attend a wine tasting seminar.

Top: Toasting with twenty-year-old wines and imported glassware brings friends together in a St. Helena home.

Above: A server lights the last candles before a wedding reception at Frank-Rombauer Cellars near Calistoga. This room was formerly used to age sparkling wine during its years as Kornell Champagne Cellars. In adjoining buildings, winemakers Koerner Rombauer and Richard Frank produce wines and provide wine storage for other wineries.

A house with a great wine stored below

lives in our imagination as a joyful house,

fast and splendidly rooted in the soil.

GEORGE MEREDITH 1828–1909

Right: Visitors to the Napa Valley Wine Auction
dine at Markham Vineyards in St. Helena. Wineries
host luncheons, dinners, and tours during the annual
June event. While temperatures averaging 58 degrees
and 90 percent humidity might not be ideal dinner
conditions, they are considered perfect for storing wine.

Tradition &

Innovation

*N*ative Americans first lived here, bestowing upon the verdant Napa Valley their word for "beautiful land." Napa Valley's customs and culture have long revolved around agriculture. A grape-growing region for more than a century, the valley was also home to less romantic and less profitable prune orchards and walnut groves. In the 1970s, the area started to reinvent itself. Today, there is innovative architecture, both wineries and private homes, where once there were simple Native American pole houses. There are orderly vineyards snaking across gentle hillocks where long ago there were empty, sprawling land grants to western settlers. Across the vineyards and inside the wineries, while science and technology point the way to more refined wines, intuition and finely tuned taste buds remain the keys to North America's best wines. New thoughts and tools and methods of growing grapes, of crafting wines, of labeling and bottling replace old ones and these, in turn, circle back to become new again. There is a resulting reverence for history and innovation alike. Under new family ownership, the grand mansion and winery buildings of Captain Gustave Niebaum, formerly Inglenook, stand much as they were a hundred years ago. Strewn along the long, narrow road that runs the length of the valley, tradition perches across from modernism, which sits next-door to neoclassic, all coexisting in a complementary mélange. With its heritage as a nurturer of life-sustaining crops, Napa Valley continues the best of its Old-World traditions in agriculture, hospitality, and community. At the beginning of the new century, it forges ahead daily to contrive better ways to make wine, to make memories for its visitors, and to make history.

Left: Quintessa wine is made from this manicured vineyard, planted by the longtime valley vintner Agustin Huneeus. The view looks south toward the Vaca Mountains bordering the eastern side of Napa Valley.

Preceding page 180: At Far Niente winery, oak barrel casks lead the way to the owner's private terrace where he entertains visitors. Meanwhile, tourists approaching Napa Valley from the south are greeted by *The Grapecrusher,* a bronze sculpture erected in 1987, by sculptor Gino Miles.

Above: Winery and vineyard owner Delia Viader uses
a refractometer to measure sugar content of grapes in
her vineyard above St. Helena. Typically, grapes for "still"
wine should have a sugar content of 22 to 23 percent.

Right: Some vineyard experts determine ripeness by
simply squeezing a grape. Softening skins indicate mature
grapes. Taste and texture are also critical.

Above: The "cap" on fermenting pinot noir grapes gets a nudge at Flora Springs Wine Company in St. Helena. This style of "open top" fermenter allows exposure to oxygen, a necessary part of the process. Fermentation gives off carbon dioxide gas, which needs to escape to allow the sugar in grape juice to convert properly into alcohol.

Right: Javier Gonzales and Felix Quesada prepare to unload a traditional basket press at Long Vineyards near St. Helena. The press squeezes the last 10 percent of the year's wine from the residue left in the fermentation vat.

Above: Traditional methods of grape crushing with feet are limited to home winemakers who may produce only a barrel or a few cases of wine annually.

Preceding pages: This method of moving grapes gently into a crusher from a stainless steel hopper requires a slow-turning auger that pulls fruit into the machinery. Stainless steel is used for most grape processing.

Above: At Louis M. Martini Winery in St. Helena, Eugenia Gomes circulates fermenting wine in a cement tank. During the fermentation process, skins will float to the top forming a "cap" which restricts oxygen from reaching the grape juice. The cap must be broken often during the ten- to twenty-day fermenting period.

Following pages: At Pride Mountain Vineyards on Spring Mountain, a winery worker shovels skins from a fermentation tank. The skins will be moved to a bladder press where the final juice will be extracted.

Wine is sunlight, held together by water!

GALILEO GALILEI 1564–1642

Right: At Schramsberg Vineyards, a bottle of sparkling wine is displayed against a wall of bottles stored in caves dug by Chinese immigrants in 1870.

Following pages 196–203: Labels from 234 wineries demonstrate the variety of shapes and colors appearing on wine bottles from Napa Valley. Unlike Europe, where wine labels have some governmental graphic restrictions and traditions, California has almost unlimited artistic boundaries.

Keenan

1998
Chardonnay
Napa Valley

PRODUCED AND BOTTLED BY ROBERT KEENAN WINERY
SPRING MTN. RD., ST. HELENA, CA. Alcohol 13.5% by Volume

DUTCH
HENRY
WINERY®

ZINFANDEL
NAPA VALLEY

1998

PRODUCED & BOTTLED BY DUTCH HENRY WINERY,
CALISTOGA CA. ALCOHOL 12.5% BY VOL.

FREEMARK
ABBEY

1995
NAPA VALLEY

CABERNET
SAUVIGNON

Sycamore Vineyards

ALCOHOL 13.5% BY VOLUME

ACACIA

SINGLE VINEYARD SELECTION

1998
DESOTO VINEYARD
PINOT NOIR
NAPA VALLEY - CARNEROS DISTRICT

SILVER OAK
1997
Alexander Valley Cabernet Sauvignon

ATLAS PEAK
VINEYARDS

1997
RESERVE
SANGIOVESE
ATLAS PEAK, NAPA VALLEY

LUNA

SANGIOVESE
1996
Napa Valley

EST 1871   VINTAGE

El Molino

NAPA VALLEY

1997   PINOT NOIR

PRODUCED AND BOTTLED BY EL MOLINO WINERY, ST. HELENA, CALIFORNIA, U.S.A.
BW-5438   ALCOHOL 14.5% BY VOLUME

SUMMIT LAKE
VINEYARDS

ESTATE BOTTLED

1996
Zinfandel
NAPA VALLEY

DOMAINE CHARBAY

1995 Napa Valley

CABERNET SAUVIGNON

St. Helena, California
Alc. 13.4% by Vol.

CARNEROS
CREEK

PALOMBO VINEYARD
CHARDONNAY
Appellation Carneros

PRODUCED & BOTTLED BY CARNEROS CREEK WINERY
NAPA, CALIFORNIA, U.S.A. ALCOHOL 12.5% BY VOLUME

ESTATE BOTTLED
1999

SMITH·MADRONE

NAPA VALLEY
RIESLING

GROWN, PRODUCED AND BOTTLED BY SMITH-MADRONE
4022 SPRING MOUNTAIN ROAD, ST. HELENA, CALIFORNIA
ALCOHOL 11.6% BY VOLUME   CONTAINS SULFITES

NAPA VALLEY
Oakville
HARLAN ESTATE

Est. 1932
ESTATE BOTTLED

REGUSCI
STAGS LEAP DISTRICT

A TRADITION OF FAMILY WINEMAKING

CABERNET SAUVIGNON
NAPA VALLEY 1998

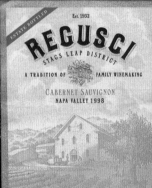

CONSTANT

Diamond
Mountain
Vineyard

1996 NAPA VALLEY

43% Cabernet Sauvignon
35% Merlot 23% Cabernet Franc

RESERVA

CAFARO

1996
NAPA VALLEY
CABERNET SAUVIGNON

STERLING
VINEYARDS

1997

Reserve
CABERNET SAUVIGNON

NAPA VALLEY
ESTATE BOTTLED

DEL DOTTO

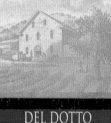

1997
NAPA VALLEY
GIOVANNI'S
TUSCAN RESERVE

PRODUCT OF U.S.A.

GUSTAVO THRACE
Zinfandel
Napa Valley
1996

J. Daniel Cuvée

Lail Vineyards

1997
NAPA VALLEY

AZALEA SPRINGS

Napa Valley
Merlot

Produced and bottled by
Azalea Springs Cellars
Oakville, California

Saviez
VINEYARDS

1997
NAPA VALLEY
Zinfandel

CABERNET SAUVIGNON

1996

NAPA VALLEY

LMR

Long Meadow Ranch

1998
BELO

B

COTTA VINEYARD
California
Vintage Port

Produced and Bottled by Belo Cellars
St. Helena, California, Alc. 19% by Vol.

GROWN, PRODUCED & BOTTLED ON THE ESTATE

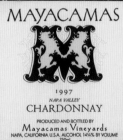

Niebaum-Coppola
Rubicon
RUTHERFORD · NAPA VALLEY
1996

1998

CUVAISON

CHARDONNAY
NAPA VALLEY · CARNEROS

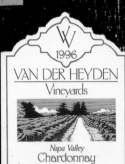

1996

VAN DER HEYDEN
Vineyards

Napa Valley
Chardonnay
ESTATE BOTTLED
GROWN AND PRODUCED BY
VAN DER HEYDEN VINEYARDS WINERY, NAPA, CA
ALCOHOL 13.5% BY VOLUME

Wermuth
Winery

NAPA VALLEY
1995
GAMAY NOIR

MAYACAMAS

1997
NAPA VALLEY
CHARDONNAY

PRODUCED AND BOTTLED BY
Mayacamas Vineyards
NAPA, CALIFORNIA U.S.A. ALCOHOL 14½% BY VOLUME   750ml

SIGNORELLO
1997 NAPA VALLEY SEMILLON
BARREL FERMENTED

Calafia
1996
CABERNET SAUVIGNON
RESERVE
NAPA VALLEY
TABLE WINE

CAYMUS
VINEYARDS
1997
NAPA VALLEY
Cabernet Sauvignon
PRODUCED AND BOTTLED BY CAYMUS VINEYARDS
RUTHERFORD, CALIFORNIA
ALCOHOL 13.5% BY VOLUME

Tudal
1997
Napa Valley
Cabernet Sauvignon
ESTATE BOTTLED
Alcohol 13.5% by vol.

1999
VILLA HELENA
NAPA VALLEY
SYRAH
Produced and bottled by Villa Helena Winery,
St. Helena, CA. Alcohol 12.6% by vol. Contains sulfites.

ANDRETTI
1997
NAPA VALLEY MERLOT

Groth
RESERVE
1997
Oakville
Cabernet Sauvignon
Napa Valley
ALC. 14.1% BY VOL.

NICHELINI
EST. 1890
1996
NAPA VALLEY
ZINFANDEL
ESTATE BOTTLED
JOSEPH A. NICHELINI
VINEYARD
ALCOHOL 14.2% BY VOLUME

Livingston
MOFFETT
1997
GEMSTONE VINEYARD
NAPA VALLEY
RED TABLE WINE
ALC. 13.7% BY VOL.

NAPA VALLEY
1998
Cabernet Sauvignon
NAPA VALLEY
ALC 13% BY VOL.
NEWLAN
VINEYARDS & WINERY

RUDD
Carneros District
CHARDONNAY
1998
PRODUCED & BOTTLED BY RUDD
OAKVILLE, CALIFORNIA
ALCOHOL 14.1% BY VOLUME
750 ML
Product of U.S.A.

1997
ESTATE
BOTTLED
STAG'S LEAP WINE CELLARS
CASK 23
RED TABLE WINE
NAPA VALLEY

PlumpJack
Cabernet Sauvignon
Reserve
1998
Oakville

Métisse
NAPA VALLEY
1997

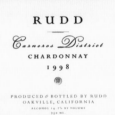
HAGAFEN
1999 Napa Valley
Pinot Noir
ALC 13.0% BY VOL.

**STORYBOOK
MOUNTAIN
VINEYARDS**
1998 ZINFANDEL
NAPA VALLEY
ESTATE RESERVE

CLOS DU VAL
1996
CABERNET SAUVIGNON
NAPA VALLEY
PRODUCED AND BOTTLED BY CLOS DU VAL WINE CO., LTD.
NAPA, CALIFORNIA USA ALCOHOL 13.5% BY VOLUME

FRAZIER
Napa Valley · Vintage 1997
CABERNET SAUVIGNON

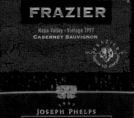
1997
JOSEPH PHELPS
INSIGNIA
NAPA
VALLEY
RED TABLE WINE

1998
AMICI
OLD VINE
ZINFANDEL
NAPA VALLEY
PICKETT VINEYARD
ALC 14.8% BY VOL.

1998
Loren Scott
VINEYARDS
Napa Valley Chardonnay

FLORA SPRINGS
1996
Napa Valley
CABERNET SAUVIGNON
St. Rutherford Vineyard
14% ALC /VOL.

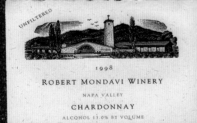
UNFILTERED
1998
ROBERT MONDAVI WINERY
NAPA VALLEY
CHARDONNAY
ALCOHOL 13.0% BY VOLUME

SKY
1997 MT. VEEDER NAPA VALLEY ZINFANDEL
TABLE WINE · ESTATE BOTTLED BY SKY VINEYARDS · NAPA CALIFORNIA

THE **HESS
COLLECTION**
NAPA VALLEY CHARDONNAY
1998
PRODUCED & BOTTLED BY THE HESS COLLECTION WINERY
NAPA, CALIFORNIA, USA
ALCOHOL 13% BY VOLUME

**LAMBORN FAMILY
VINEYARDS**
NAPA VALLEY
HOWELL MOUNTAIN
ZINFANDEL
1997
The Team Connection
GROWN BY LAMBORN FAMILY VINEYARDS, ANGWIN, CA.
PRODUCED AND BOTTLED BY LAMBORN FAMILY WINE COMPANY, OAKVILLE, CA.
ALCOHOL 14.5% BY VOLUME   CONTAINS SULFITES

NAPA VALLEY
Silverado
VINEYARDS
SANGIOVESE

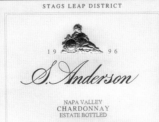
STAGS LEAP DISTRICT
1996
S. Anderson
NAPA VALLEY
CHARDONNAY
ESTATE BOTTLED
WHITE TABLE WINE

Carneros
PINOT NOIR
1999
SAINTSBURY
PRODUCED AND BOTTLED BY SAINTSBURY
NAPA, CALIFORNIA, USA   ALCOHOL 13.5% BY VOLUME

HONIG
NAPA VALLEY
CABERNET SAUVIGNON
1998

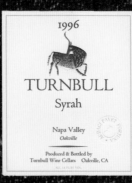

Prager
California
Tawny
Summer Port
CELLARED AND BOTTLED BY
PRAGER WINERY & PORT WORKS
ST. HELENA, CALIFORNIA
ALCOHOL 18% BY VOLUME

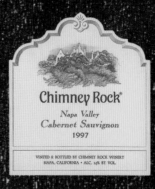

1996
TURNBULL
Syrah
Napa Valley
Oakville
Produced & Bottled by
Turnbull Wine Cellars   Oakville, CA

Chimney Rock®
Napa Valley
Cabernet Sauvignon
1997
VINTED & BOTTLED BY CHIMNEY ROCK WINERY
NAPA, CALIFORNIA • ALC. 14% BY VOL.

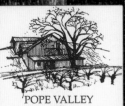

POPE VALLEY
1998
MERLOT
ESTATE BOTTLED
NAPA VALLEY
PRODUCED & BOTTLED BY POPE VALLEY WINERY
POPE VALLEY, CALIFORNIA
ALC. 14.0% BY VOLUME

QUIXOTE
1997
NAPA VALLEY RED WINE
61% Merlot, 31% Cabernet Franc,
and 9% Cabernet Sauvignon
ALCOHOL 12.5% BY VOLUME

1998
SEQUOIA
GROVE
Cabernet Sauvignon
Napa Valley
PRODUCED & BOTTLED BY
SEQUOIA GROVE VINEYARDS
RUTHERFORD, CA USA ALCOHOL 13.8% BY VOL.
A Kobrand
Corporation   California
Selection

Benessere
1998
NAPA VALLEY SANGIOVESE

Abreu
Cabernet Sauvignon
Napa Valley   1997

VILLA
MT. EDEN
Grand Reserve
CHARDONNAY

PETER MICHAEL
WINERY
1998
'BELLE CÔTE'
SONOMA COUNTY CHARDONNAY • ALCOHOL 14.5% BY VOLUME
ESTATE BOTTLED BY PETER MICHAEL
CALISTOGA, CA USA

RESERVE
1997
M
MARKHAM
VINEYARDS
Merlot
NAPA VALLEY
ALC. 14.5% BY VOL.

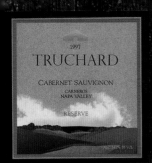

1997
TRUCHARD
CABERNET SAUVIGNON
CARNEROS
NAPA VALLEY
RESERVE
ALC. 14% BY VOL.

RESERVE
1998
BEAUCANON
NAPA VALLEY
Merlot
ESTATE GROWN
PRODUCED & BOTTLED BY BEAUCANON WINERY, ST. HELENA, CA

Chase
ST. HELENA
HAYNE VINEYARD 1998 ZINFANDEL
ALC. 15.2% BY VOL.

Mario Perelli-Minetti®
100%
1998
Napa Valley
CHARDONNAY
PRODUCED AND BOTTLED BY M.P.M. VINEYARDS,
RUTHERFORD, CA   ALCOHOL 14.2% BY VOLUME

M. TRINCHERO®
FOUNDER'S ESTATE
cabernet sauvignon
1997 NAPA VALLEY

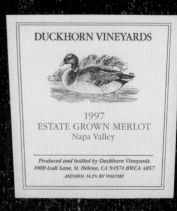

DUCKHORN VINEYARDS
1997
ESTATE GROWN MERLOT
Napa Valley
Produced and bottled by Duckhorn Vineyards
1000 Lodi Lane, St. Helena, CA 94574 BWCA 4857
ALCOHOL 14.2% BY VOLUME

RITCHIE CREEK
1998
Cabernet Sauvignon
Napa Valley
Spring Mountain District
ALC. 13.2% BY VOL.

SUTTER
HOME®
PINOT NOIR

STONY HILL
NAPA VALLEY
CHARDONNAY
1996
Grown, produced and bottled 600 feet
above the floor of the Napa Valley by
Stony Hill Vineyard, St. Helena, Calif.
ALCOHOL 13% BY VOLUME CONTAINS SULFITES

CHAPPELLET
Donn Chappellet
1997
Napa Valley
Cabernet Sauvignon
GROWN,
PRODUCED
AND BOTTLED
BY CHAPPELLET
VINEYARD
ST. HELENA
CA. U.S.A.
B.W. 4507
ALC. 14.3% BY VOL.

CABERNET SAUVIGNON
19 96
ESTATE
BUEHLER
VINEYARDS

FROG'S LEAP
1999 SAUVIGNON BLANC
NAPA VALLEY
PRODUCED & BOTTLED BY FROG'S LEAP, RUTHERFORD, CA

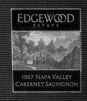

EDGEWOOD
ESTATE
1997 NAPA VALLEY
CABERNET SAUVIGNON

ESTATE
David Arthur
NAPA VALLEY
Elevation 1147

19 98
ROBERT SINSKEY VINEYARDS
PINOT NOIR
LOS CARNEROS OF NAPA VALLEY
2ND BARRELS PRODUCED
GROWN, PRODUCED & BOTTLED BY ROBERT SINSKEY VINEYARDS
NAPA, CALIFORNIA USA • ALC. 13.2% BY VOL.

BALLENTINE
1995
NAPA VALLEY
Merlot
ESTATE GROWN

199

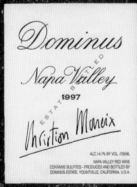

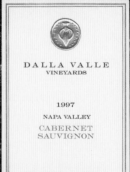

200

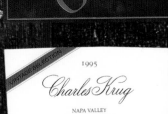

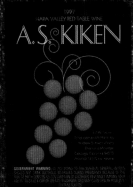

Zahtila Vineyards
ZINFANDEL
Napa Valley
1998
ESTATE BOTTLED
ALC. 13.9% BY VOL.

FIRST
MAX
CUVÉE
NAPA VALLEY

The Cat's Meow
1994
Napa Valley
Zinfandel
Compliments of Bill & Lois Hopkins,
St. Helena, Napa County, California

EMMOLO
MERLOT
1998 NAPA VALLEY

THE
TERRACES
1996
NAPA VALLEY
CABERNET
SAUVIGNON
PRODUCED AND BOTTLED BY
W. HOGUE VINTNERS
RUTHERFORD, CALIFORNIA
ALCOHOL 13.6% BY VOLUME
CONTAINS SULFITES

1997
ANDERSON'S
Conn Valley Vineyards
NAPA VALLEY
Pinot Noir
VALHALLA VINEYARD
PRODUCED AND BOTTLED BY CONN VALLEY VINEYARDS
ST. HELENA, CALIFORNIA • ALCOHOL 13.2% BY VOLUME

VIVIANI
VINEYARDS
1997
CABERNET
SAUVIGNON
NAPA VALLEY
VINTED & BOTTLED BY VIVIANI VINEYARDS, OAKVILLE, CA
ALC. 14.2% BY VOLUME

Quail Ridge
NAPA VALLEY
Napa Valley
Cabernet Sauvignon
1998

Beaulieu Vineyard
SINCE BV 1900
Georges De Latour
Private Reserve
CABERNET SAUVIGNON
NAPA VALLEY
1996
PRODUCED & BOTTLED BY BEAULIEU VINEYARD
RUTHERFORD, CALIFORNIA

Estate Bottled
1997
SPRING MOUNTAIN
VINEYARD
Miravalle - La Perla - Chevalier
No. 02265
of 87,861 Bottles
Director
Thomas Ferrell
A Napa Valley Red Wine

RICHARD PERRY
Napa Valley
1997
CABERNET SAUVIGNON
PERRY VINEYARDS

TULOCAY
Chiles Valley 1998
NAPA VALLEY
ZINFANDEL

GRGICH HILLS
Napa Valley
CHARDONNAY
1997
PRODUCED AND BOTTLED BY GRGICH HILLS CELLAR
RUTHERFORD, CA • ALC. 13.4% BY VOL • CONTAINS SULFITES

SWANSON
1998
NAPA VALLEY
MERLOT
GROWN, VINTED AND BOTTLED BY
SWANSON VINEYARDS RUTHERFORD
CA 94573 • ALC 14.1% BY VOL

Richard
Partridge
1998
CABERNET SAUVIGNON
NAPA VALLEY

Madonna Estate
MONT St JOHN
Chardonnay
CARNEROS 1998

NAPA VALLEY CHARDONNAY
DARIOUSH

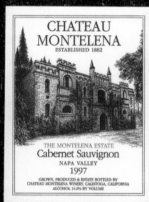

CHATEAU
MONTELENA
ESTABLISHED 1882
THE MONTELENA ESTATE
Cabernet Sauvignon
NAPA VALLEY
1997
GROWN, PRODUCED & ESTATE BOTTLED BY
CHATEAU MONTELENA WINERY, CALISTOGA, CALIFORNIA
ALCOHOL 14.0% BY VOLUME

ROMBAUER
VINEYARDS
Carneros
CHARDONNAY
VINTED AND BOTTLED BY ROMBAUER VINEYARDS
ST. HELENA, CALIFORNIA • ALCOHOL 15.8% BY VOLUME

Vintage 1999

Far Niente
ESTABLISHED 1885
ESTATE BOTTLED
1997
NAPA VALLEY
Cabernet Sauvignon
PRODUCED AND BOTTLED BY FAR NIENTE WINERY
OAKVILLE, CALIFORNIA, USA
ALCOHOL 13.9% BY VOLUME
NICKEL & NICKEL, PROPRIETORS

VINTAGE 1998
Etude
Pinot Noir
CARNEROS
THIS WINE WAS CELLARED AND BOTTLED BY ETUDE WINES
RUTHERFORD, CALIFORNIA • ALCOHOL 13.5% BY VOLUME

ESTATE BOTTLED
PARADIGM
1996
NAPA VALLEY
Cabernet Sauvignon
OAKVILLE

RUTHERFORD
HILL
Twenty Fourth Anniversary
1995
CHARDONNAY
NAPA VALLEY
ALCOHOL 13.5% BY VOLUME

1997
MONTICELLO
CORLEY FAMILY VINEYARDS
Merlot
NAPA VALLEY

GALLERON
NAPA VALLEY 1998 MORISOLI VINEYARD
Cabernet Sauvignon

VINTAGE 1995
Bottle
Magnum
BOTTLED APRIL 1999
of a total of 54,348 Bottles
of a total of 1200 Magnums

MUMM
CUVÉE NAPA
Napa Valley • California
BRUT PRESTIGE
METHODE CHAMPENOISE
NAPA VALLEY SPARKLING WINE
750 ML (25.4 FL OZ.)
ALC. 12.5% BY VOL.

Long
Vineyards
1995
ESTATE GROWN NAPA VALLEY
CABERNET SAUVIGNON

CABERNET SAUVIGNON NAPA VALLEY
colgin
1997
HERB LAMB VINEYARD
13.5% alcohol by volume

Heitz Cellar
NAPA VALLEY
CABERNET SAUVIGNON
ALCOHOL 13.5% BY VOLUME
BELLA OAKS VINEYARD
PRODUCED AND BOTTLED IN OUR CELLAR BY
HEITZ WINE CELLARS
ST. HELENA, CALIFORNIA, U.S.A.

CHATEAU POTELLE
1997
CABERNET SAUVIGNON
MT. VEEDER
NAPA VALLEY

Shypoke
CHARBONO
1998
Napa Valley

1 9 9 6
ONE
NAPA VALLEY
Vineyard and Winery
CABERNET SAUVIGNON

Rosenblum
CELLARS
1998
NAPA VALLEY
Petite Sirah
Pickett Road
ALCOHOL 13.6% BY VOLUME

ASTRALE e TERRA
Napa Valley
CABERNET
SAUVIGNON
1997

Guenoc
BECKSTOFFER IV VINEYARD
NAPA VALLEY
1997 CABERNET SAUVIGNON
RESERVE · RESERVE

LA SIRENA
1997
SANGIOVESE
NAPA VALLEY
Jeltjen Vineyard
PRODUCED & BOTTLED BY LA SIRENA, OAKVILLE, CA
ALC. 14.1% BY VOL.

Philippe-Lorraine
1997
Napa Valley Cabernet Sauvignon
Philippe Lorraine Winery
Oakville, California

PHILLIP BAXTER, PROPRIETOR
APPELLATION NAPA VALLEY
PRODUCT OF U.S.A.   ALC. 14.3% BY VOL.

1997
RISTOW
ESTATE
Cabernet Sauvignon
Quinta de Pedras Vineyard
Napa Valley

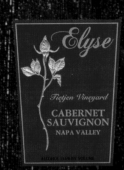

Elyse
Tietjen Vineyard
CABERNET
SAUVIGNON
NAPA VALLEY
ALCOHOL 13.5% BY VOLUME

ESTABLISHED 1973
STONEGATE
NAPA VALLEY
Cabernet Sauvignon
1997

ELAN
VINEYARDS
CABERNET SAUVIGNON
NAPA VALLEY ATLAS PEAK
ALCOHOL 13.5% BY VOLUME

ELKHORN PEAK
1998
Napa Valley
PINOT NOIR
Fagan Creek Vineyard

BOUCHAINE
CHARDONNAY
CARNEROS
NAPA VALLEY
1998
ALCOHOL 13% BY VOLUME

Snowden
NAPA VALLEY
CABERNET SAUVIGNON
1998

STAGLIN FAMILY
VINEYARD
CABERNET SAUVIGNON
RUTHERFORD, NAPA VALLEY
1997
PRODUCED & BOTTLED BY STAGLIN FAMILY VINEYARD, OAKVILLE, CA   750ML   13.8% BY VOL.

Destino
CHARDONNAY
NAPA VALLEY

WHITE COTTAGE
SINCE 1890
VINTAGE
1997
Cabernet
Sauvignon
HOWELL MOUNTAIN
NAPA VALLEY
ALC. 13.4% BY VOL

KONGSGAARD
NAPA VALLEY · CHARDONNAY · VINTAGE 1999

PALOMA
NAPA VALLEY
MERLOT

Lewelling
VINEYARDS
1997
CABERNET SAUVIGNON
WIGHT VINEYARD
St Helena · Napa Valley

L

ALTAMURA
1997
Sangiovese

Madrigal
1995
Napa Valley
Petite Sirah
PRODUCED AND BOTTLED BY MADRIGAL VINEYARDS
OAKVILLE, CALIFORNIA. 14% ALCOHOL BY VOLUME

SUMMERS
Knights Valley
MERLOT
1997
ALCOHOL 13.5% BY VOLUME

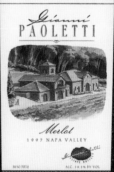

Gianni
PAOLETTI
Merlot
1997 NAPA VALLEY
ALC. 14.1% BY VOL.

RESERVE
CABERNET SAUVIGNON

JARVIS
1996
ESTATE GROWN
CAVE FERMENTED
Cabernet Sauvignon
NAPA VALLEY
William Jarvis, Owner   Dimitri Tchelistcheff, Winemaker

LANG & REED
Wild Hare Rosé
Cabernet Franc
NAPA VALLEY

HARTWELL
VINEYARDS
NAPA VALLEY
STAGS LEAP DISTRICT
Cabernet Sauvignon
The Hartwell Estate Sunshine Vineyard is planted on rocky,
steep and terraced hillside terrain in the famous microclimate of
the Stags Leap District in the Napa Valley and produces this
excellent Cabernet Sauvignon wine.
VINTED AND BOTTLED BY
HARTWELL VINEYARDS
NAPA, CALIFORNIA
SUNSHINE VINEYARD

Graeser
1996
CABERNET FRANC
Napa Valley
ESTATE BOTTLED

DAWSON   CRAIG
Killam   MacLean
WINEMAKERS
CABERNET SAUVIGNON
Alcohol 13.5% By Volume   Oakville, Napa Valley

WILSON DANIELS
1 9 9 7
Chardonnay
California

MASON
1997
NAPA VALLEY
MERLOT
ALCOHOL 13.8% BY VOLUME

Dusinberre
1998
Napa Valley
CABERNET SAUVIGNON
VINTED AND BOTTLED BY DUSINBERRE CELLARS
ST. HELENA, CA. ALCOHOL 13.4% BY VOLUME   750 ML
WWW.MISSICAL.COM   (707) 942-4584

Left and above: Shadows are cast across sleek, contemporary furniture in this "Modernist-minimalist" tasting room at Artesa Winery west of Napa. In the tasting room of Beringer Vineyards *(above)* in St. Helena, where style was defined differently one hundred years ago, glasses are arranged for tour guests who will arrive shortly from the caves located behind the historic seventeen-room mansion.

Preceding pages: Cabernet sauvignon's opaque characteristics distinguish it from other wines, as seen in this informal portrait.

Following pages: Warm light flows through an original stained glass window created for the Rhine House at Beringer Vineyards. Hunting scenes like this one appear in the grand staircase landing window *(pages 208–209)*. Echoing the effect of stained glass, light flows through the rock walls of Dominus Estate. The eighteen-inch walls of basalt are contained in eighteen-inch by twelve-foot steel cage "gabions." Workers spent six months hand loading 1,203 cages with 3,000 metric tons of the rock *(pages 210–211)*.

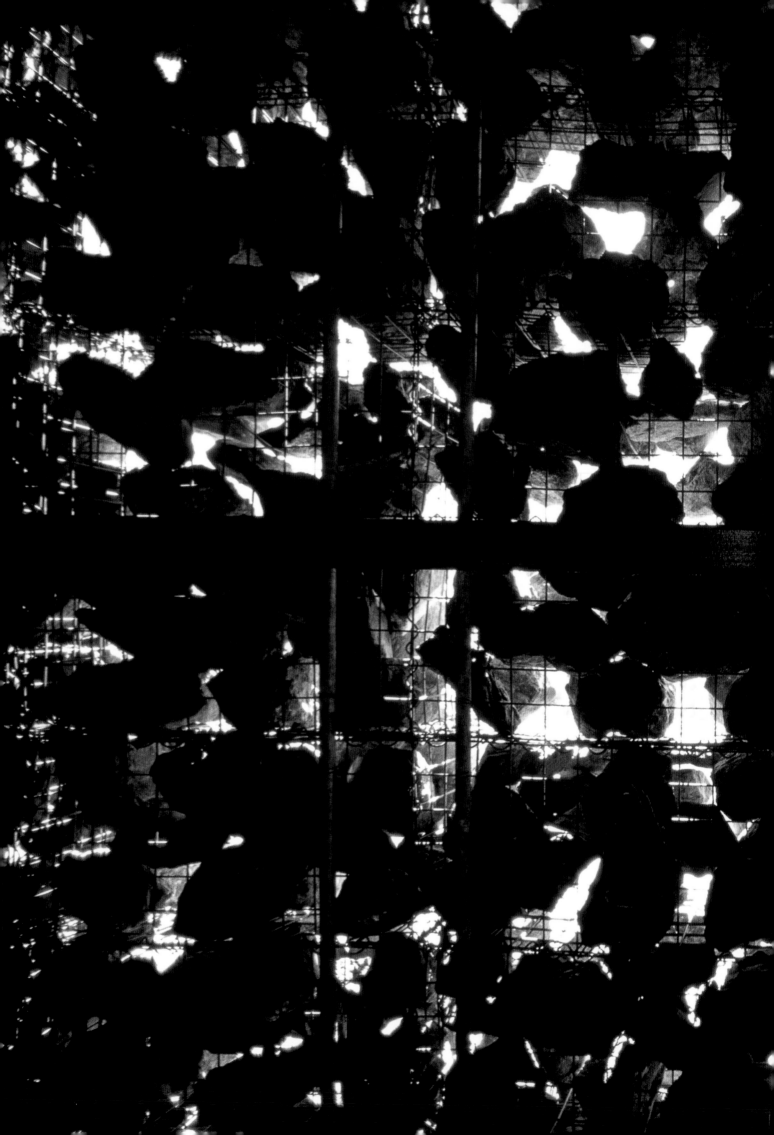

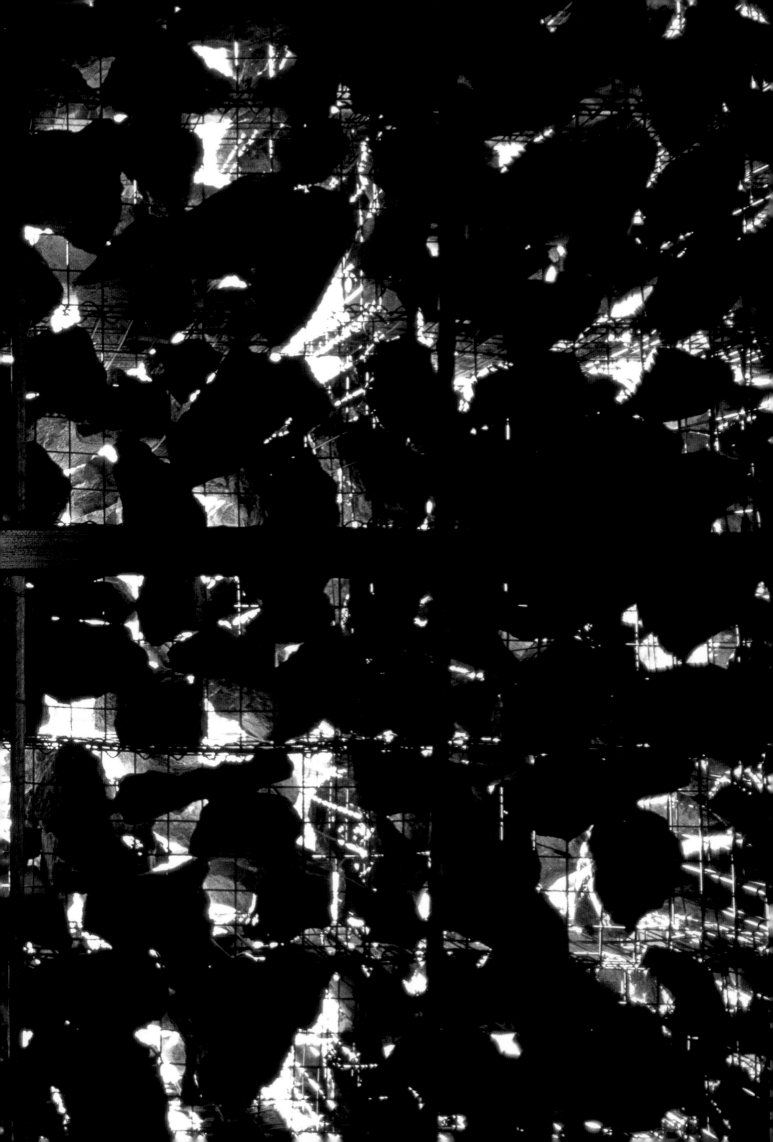

Left: Architecture designed to resemble buildings on the Greek island of Mykonos accents the hilltop winery of Sterling Vineyards. The winery was built in 1972 on a three hundred-foot knoll south of Calistoga. The tower's bells were salvaged from a London church that had been destroyed during World War II.

Above: Architecture from another faraway place—South Africa—shows traditional Cape Dutch style at Chimney Rock Winery north of Napa.

Following pages: From the rooftop terrace of Opus One winery in Oakville, well-defined rows of grapes appear to vanish toward Highway 29 in the distance.

Long life to the grape!

For when summer is flown,

the age of our nectar

shall gladden our own.

Right: A portrait of Cabernet Sauvignon wine against a background of cabernet sauvignon grapes from the vineyard of David Abreu in St. Helena.

Preceding pages: Wild mustard signals the approach of spring at the Rossi Vineyard along Highway 29 south of St. Helena.

Following pages: Rolling hills of vines dominate the landscape in the Carneros region west of Napa. The region grows primarily chardonnay and pinot noir grapes because of the influence of cool and moist weather from nearby San Francisco Bay *(pages 220–221).* Native fir trees on Spring Mountain appear above the valley fog. Ocean proximity creates a moist climate on the western slopes of Napa Valley in contrast to the valley's eastern slopes only five miles in the distance, where dry and, in some places, almost desertlike conditions exist *(pages 222–223).* A celestial celebration over a cabernet vineyard in St. Helena ends another day in the Napa Valley *(pages 224–225).*

Napa Valley Grape Growers

Some residents describe Napa Valley's independent grape growers as the backbone of the wine industry. They receive little public recognition and are usually known only to their nearest neighbor, or to the winery where they sell grapes. Many of them prefer to be known as farmers; a few can be called "gentlemen farmers."

Since winemaking began in the valley more than 100 years ago, growers have traditionally owned their land, prepared the soil, planted the grapes, and delivered the product to the winery. A grower's style of farming is reflected in the quality and flavor of grapes.

More recently wineries have made strong efforts to own and control their own vineyards—and hire their own managers. Still, the grape grower continues to play an important role. Ancestors of many growers came to the valley from Europe, while others began grape growing as a second profession.

Miles Alexander, born 1919
Grows six acres of cabernet. Retired from Mare Island naval shipyard. *p. 50*

Bill Ballentine & daughter Claire, born 1963 & 1997
Great-grandparents of Bill came from Tuscany in 1906 and planted grapes in Calistoga. He is a winemaker who grows two acres of cabernet in St. Helena. *p. 56*

Bob Barbaris, born 1935
Grandparents came from Italy in 1900. Grocery store owner until early 1970s, then took over father's vineyard. At 14 started working in vineyard. Grows mostly cabernet on 40 acres near Calistoga. *p. 54*

Dorothy & Benito Barbozza, both born 1919
His Spanish parents came to Napa Valley in 1921. He first worked in a vineyard at age 10. They own 17 acres. *p. 54*

Bill Bartolucci, born 1946
Grows 150 acres of different varieties. Lifelong grape grower. *p. 55*

Bruno Bartolucci, born 1920
Parents came from near Rimini, Italy. Grows 175 acres of grapes near St. Helena, mostly cabernet sauvignon. Retired steelworker at Mare Island Naval Shipyard. *p. 9*

Craig Battuello, born 1946
Grandfather came to Napa Valley in 1909. Planted first vineyard at age 13. Grows 70 acres of cabernet and zinfandel. Photographed holding his favorite 50-year-old smudge pot. *p. 55*

Andy Beckstoffer, born 1939
Came to Napa Valley in 1969 as winery executive. Owns and farms on more than 1000 acres of vineyards, mostly cabernet. *p. 50*

Aldo Biale, born 1929
Parents came from Italy in 1920s, met and married in Napa. Grows 25 acres of grapes. *p. 50*

Soren Bloch, born 1941
Grown grapes since 1982, mostly zinfandel. Grows 2 acres of grapes. Airline pilot. *p. 154*

Keith Bowers, born 1924
Has grown grapes since 1957. Grows 5 acres merlot. Retired Napa County vineyard farm adviser. *p. 51*

Chester Brandlin, born 1923
Grandfather came from Switzerland in 1870s. Helped father in vineyard since age four. Grows 4 varities on 15 acres on Mt. Veeder above Napa. Holds hazel branch used for dowsing water. *p. 50*

Grant Cairns, born 1920
Great-grandparents came to Napa Valley in 1874. Grows 75 acres of zinfandel. Retired from Air Force. Holds photo of his father. *p. 51*

Lewis Carpenter, born 1916
Planted first grapes in 1946. Grows 125 acres near St. Helena. Retired clinical psychologist. *p. 55*

Ed Chaix, born 1925
Grandparents came from France in 1909. Has grown grapes since family moved from San Francisco in 1937. Grows 37 acres of cabernet, chardonnay, and zinfandel. Retired fire chief of Rutherford. *p. 50*

Rene di Rosa, born 1919
Retired newspaper reporter. Farmed 250 acres for 35 years, and sold the vineyards in 1990. Owns di Rosa Preserve: Art and Nature in Carneros district. *p. 55*

Roy Enderlin, born 1925
Grandparents came from Germany. Bought land in 1952. Former prune grower. Now grows 3 varieties of grapes on 18 acres near Calistoga. *p. 54*

James Frediani, born 1951
With his mother, Jeanne, grows 13 varieties on 150 acres near Calistoga. *p. 52*

Jim Haire, Born 1942
Planted first grapes in 1977. Grows 50 acres of pinot noir and chardonnay in Carneros region. Farmed all his life. *p. 55*

Michael, Bill & John Muir Hanna, born 1972, 1945 & 1909
Direct descendants of naturalist John Muir. They own 40 acres and manage 93 acres in the Dry Creek area near Napa. *p. 57*

Otty Hayne, born 1925
Inherited his land from his great-grandparents. Grows 4 varieties on 52 acres near St. Helena. Holds zinfandel vine planted by father in 1905. Former mayor of St. Helena. Retired foreign service officer. *p. 50*

Andrew Hoxsey, born 1955
Fourth-generation grape grower. Great-grandparents came in late 1800s from Genoa, Italy. Grows 600 acres and sells 13 varieties to 21 wineries. Career grape grower. *p. 51*

Edgar Ilsley, born 1936
Grandfather came from England. Father worked in vineyard. Started growing grapes 1953. Sons David (99) and Ernie help with grape growing on their 37 acres near Yountville. *p. 54*

Lindy Johnson, born 1944
Parents planted grapes in nearby Alexander Valley in 1960s. Grows 3 varieties on 25 acres near Calistoga. Nurse-midwife in Berkeley and commutes to her vineyard in Napa Valley. *p. 51*

Robert Keig, born 1944
Grandfather grew grapes and prunes in Napa Valley. Grows 35 acres of grapes, mostly merlot and zinfandel. Kindergarten teacher. *p. 53*

Dr. Tom Kenefick, born 1935
Grows 4 varieties on 125 acres near Calistoga. Photographed after plowing vineyard. Neurosurgeon. *p. 159*

Ted Laurent, born 1913
Ancestors came to gold rush from France in 1850s. Born on the property where he grows 4 varieties on 30 acres. Grandfather built what is now Markham Winery. Retired boiler maker at Kaiser Steel. *p. 158*

Ira Lee, born 1921
Bought weekend home in Carneros in 1966 and planted vineyard in 1967. Grows 35 acres of chardonnay and pinot noir. Retired contractor. *p. 54*

William Lincoln, Sr., born 1916
Moved to Napa Valley in 1964, planted first grapes in 1973. Grows primarily cabernet and merlot on 13 acres. Retired airline pilot and engineer. *p. 54*

Fred Lyon, born 1924
Since 1972 has grown 7 acres of cabernet along Silverado Trail. Former *Life* magazine photographer. Professional photographer in San Francisco. *p. 54*

Thomas & Martha May
Grow 35 acres of cabernet in Oakville. Owners of Martha's Vineyard, first vineyard to be recognized on wine label. *p. 51*

Joe Miller, born 1939
Owns 345 acres near Yountville. Leases 300 acres and grows 45 acres of mostly merlot. Planted first grapes 1963. *p. 54*

Mike Morisoli, born 1969
Manages his mother's two-and-one-half-acre cabernet vineyard. Geotechnical engineer. *p. 51*

Ernie Navone, born 1922
Parents came from Asti and Torino, Italy. Helped father in vineyards beginning at age 10. Grows 8 acres of cabernet, 2 acres of petite sirah. Retired butcher. *p. 51*

Linda & Mike Neal,
born 1956 & 1957
Own 5 acres of cabernet. Professional vineyard managers. *p. 54*

Joseph Nichelini, born 1931
Worked in vineyard since child. Grows 6 varieties on 100 acres in Chiles Valley, east of St. Helena. Stockbroker. *p. 17*

Osvaldo Particelli, born 1924
Born in Italy. Owner of Napa Valley Olive Oil Mfg. Company since 1963. Grows 7 acres of cabernet. *p. 54*

Frank Perata, born 1933
Grandparents came from Italy. Grows 46 acres of zinfandel, chardonnay, and cabernet. His son David now manages vineyard. *p. 55*

Lucio "Cio" Perez, born 1952
Grandfather came from Jalisco, Mexico, in 1935. Joined family grape growing business in 1976. Grows 35 acres of chardonnay, zinfandel and cabernet, and manages 70 acres of mostly cabernet. *p. 55*

Earle Presten, born 1937
Grows 3 acres of petite sirah Blue-ribbon home winemaker. Retired airline pilot. *p. 51*

Angelo Regusci, born 1926
Parents came from Southern Switzerland. Grows 7 acres of zinfandel, 12 acres of chardonnay, five acres of pinot noir grapes. Former cattle rancher. *p. 51*

Salvador & Oscar Renteria,
born 1938 & 1967
Grow 100 acres, mostly cabernet. Professional managers of 1,200 acres. Oscar started tying vines at age 10. Salvador came from Jalisco, Mexico, in 1962. *p. 50*

Belle & Barney Rhodes, born 1920
Planted grapes 1954, 17 acres of cabernet used exclusively in "Bella Oaks" cabernet. He is a retired dermatologist with U.S. Navy. She is a retired occupational therapist. *p. 50*

Paul Rolleri, born 1920
Father born in Italy; mother born in Napa Valley. Grows one and one-half acres of zinfandel. Former carpenter. *p. 54*

Andrew Rossi, born 1922
Parents came from the Bergamo region of Italy. Grows 5 acres petite sirah, mostly planted in 1905. Holds pruning shears that trim an average of 3,000 vines yearly. Retired steel inspector. *p. 39*

James St. Clair, born 1920
Came to Carneros region 1966. Grows 9 acres of pinot noir. Retired surveyor from Mare Island shipyard. *p. 51*

Paul Saviez, born 1954
Grandfather came to Napa Valley from France. Grows 160 acres of grapes. Professional vineyard manager. *p. 50*

Randy & Scott Snowden,
born 1949 & 1946
Parents bought 23 acres in 1955 near St. Helena. The brothers planted 4 varieties of grapes in 1980. Scott is a Superior Court judge. Randy is a human services administrator. *p. 156*

Bruno Solari, born 1958
Grandfather came from Tuscany. Manages for his family 3 varieties on 110 acres near Calistoga. Began tying vines in vineyard at age 14. *p. 155*

Frank Takahashi, born 1918
Bought land 1973, planted first vines 1975. Grows 5 varieties on 70 acres. Grows bonsai plants as hobby. Retired Chicago accountant. *p. 51*

Dr. James Talcott, born 1940
Planted first vines 1975. Grows 4 varieties on 100 acres. Photographed with dogs, Roxy and Reina. Orthopedic surgeon. *p. 51*

Ted Tamagni, born 1958
Grandparents came from Italy. Involved in grape growing since a child. Grows 3 varieties on 62 acres near Calistoga. Heavy equipment mechanic. *p. 157*

Henry "Irv" Tiedemann, born 1922
Grandfather came from Germany and bought land in 1887 where his vineyard and house are now. Grows 8 acres of zinfandel. Photographed with horse collar he used as teenager to plow father's vineyard. *p. 50*

Pauline Tofanelli, born 1924
Father came from Italy in 1910. With her sister May grows 30 acres of charbono, semillon, sauvignon blanc, and zinfandel near Calistoga. *p. 48*

Lou "Botch" Tonella, born 1912
Parents came to Napa Valley from Italy. Started with Beaulieu Vineyard in 1929. In 1948 bought first vineyard, grows 50 acres of cabernet, chardonnay, cabernet franc, and merlot. *p. 50*

Sloan Upton, born 1936
Planted first grapes 1968. He and brother John farm 5 grape varieties on 83 acres between St. Helena and Calistoga. Began career as vineyard manager. *p. 54*

Arn Vallerga, born 1931
Parents came to Napa Valley from Italy in 1949. Grows 30 acres of cabernet. Retired utility company foreman. *p. 55*

Harold Varozza, born 1927
Grandparents came from near the Swiss-Italian border. Father born in St. Helena 1882. Grows 40 acres of grapes with son, Jack. Construction company owner. *p. 55*

Alex Vyborny, born 1947
Came to Napa Valley in 1972 after his education in viticulture. Owns 100 acres. Manages 1,700 acres. *p. 55*

Charles Wagner, born 1912
Born in Rutherford near where he started Caymus Winery. Parents came from Alsace (Germany) in 1885. Last worked in vineyards in 1975. At peak in 1950s he owned 75 acres of vines. *p. 50*

Wes Walker, born 1933
With wife, Susan, grows 3 acres of cabernet. Justice, Court of Appeals of California, San Francisco. *p. 55*

Frank "Laurie" Wood, born 1920
Grows on 87 acres and manages 250 acres. Has dowsed 1,000 wells as well seeker. *p. 55*

This edition published in 2001 by Wineviews Publishing LLC, Box 361 St. Helena, California 94574 Tel: 707-963-2663 Photographs from this book are available for sale and can be seen at www.wineviews.com.

Distributed in Australia by Simon & Schuster Australia, in Canada by Ten Speed Press Canada, in New Zealand by Southern Publishers Group, in South Africa by Real Books, in Southeast Asia by Berkeley Books, and in the United Kingdom and Europe by Airlift Book Company.

Produced by
Jennifer Barry Design, Sausalito, California and Charles O'Rear St. Helena, California
Design, Jennifer Barry
Editing, Blake Hallanan
Layout production, Kristen Wurz
Project coordination, Jane Ballentine
Proofreading, Barbara King

ISBN 1-58008-322-6
Library of Congress information on file with publisher
Printed in Hong Kong

Wineviews Publishing LLC, St. Helena, California
Ten Speed Press, Berkeley/Toronto

Acknowledgments

Inspiration and strength for monumental projects like this come from daily thoughts of those who love me unconditionally—my son Michael who cannot know the taste of great wine nor can he walk a vineyard, my extraordinary sweetheart Daphne Larkin, my parents, Homer and Ada, and my daughter Stephanie.

A book of this scope requires the support and ideas from many friends. It requires support from a community where people cooperate and share. It requires support from growers who now feel like family, and the hundreds of wineries that graciously opened their doors. This book represents the best of my wine photography and the best of Napa Valley from more than twenty-two years of work.

My interest in wine, and particularly Napa Valley, took on new meaning when two editors introduced me to this valley. I have great admiration and respect for *National Geographic's* editor Bill Garrett and his wife, Lucy, and to the photography director Bob Gilka and his wife, Janet.

To others who gave: David Abreu, Christina Adamson, Jerry and Loma Alexander, Bill Allen, John Aquila, Daphne and Bart Araujo, Roger Asleson, Craig and Daphne Aurness, Mary Azevedo, Bill and Jane Ballentine, Andy Beckstoffer, Sandi Belcher, Larry Bentinelli, Michael and Arlene Bernstein, Carole Bidnick, Tracy Brash and Rebecca Kingsley, Dona Kopol Bonick, Denice Britton, Chris Burt, Mike Carpenter, Ann Marie Conover, Michael Creedman, Jim and Sue Cross, Brother Timothy Diener, Cate Coniff Dobrich, Dawnine and Bill Dwyer, Jennifer Erwitt and Rick Smolan, Macduff Everton and Mary Hebner, Elias Fernandez, Bruce Fleming, Kathryn Fowler, Lucie Morton Garrett, Dick and Ann Grace, Dan Gustafson, Mark Heinemann, Steve Hix, Jerry Hyde, Chris Howell, Dennis Johns, Tor and Susan Kenward, Tony Knickerbocker, Bob and Peggy Krist, Herb and Jennifer Lamb, Robin and Jon Lail, Bruce LeFavour, Ian Lloyd, Bob Long, Regina Lutz, Carolyn Martini, Paul Mason, Jean-Marie Maureze, Rob McMillan, Peter Menzel, Bob and Margrit Mondavi, Holli Morton, Christian and Cherise Moueix, Mary Novak, Jim O'Shea, Kelly Osmundsen, Leonora Particelli, Chris Phelps, Françoise Peschon, Isaac and Eteluina Perez, Jean Phillips, Earle and Valerie Presten, Julie Prince, Michael Raymor, Giovanni Scala, Jan Shrem, Michael Silacci, Bettina Sichel, Meg Smith, Stu Smith, Bob Steinhauer, Lorin and Edy and John Sorensen, Lily and Charles Thomas, Peter Venutra and Melissa Wolfe, Larry Vermillion, Helene Weiss, Leslie Wilks, Warren Winiarski, Ira Wolk, and Laurie Wood.

Special attention for this project came from the The Darkroom photo lab of Reseda, California, from the black and white photo lab of David Spindler in San Francisco, and from the New Lab of San Francisco.

To those I may have accidentally omitted, please forgive me.